T0145001

Don't Worry, Worship Worship, Don't Worry

VERNADETTE R. AUGUSTUSEL

WESTBOW
PRESS®
A DIVISION OF THOMAS NELSON
& ZONDERVAN

Unless otherwise indicated, all scripture quotations are from:
The Holy Bible: New International Version, © 1973, 1978, and 1984 by the International Bible Society. Used by permission of Zondervan.

Amplified Bible (AMP) Copyright © 1954, 1958, 1962, 1964, 1965, 1987 Zondervan Corporation, the Lockman Foundation. All rights reserved.

This book is a work of non-fiction. Unless otherwise noted, the author and the publisher make no explicit guarantees as to the accuracy of the information contained in this book and in some cases, names of people and places have been altered to protect their privacy.

WestBow Press books may be ordered through booksellers or by contacting:

WestBow Press
A Division of Thomas Nelson & Zondervan
1663 Liberty Drive
Bloomington, IN 47403
www.westbowpress.com
1 (866) 928-1240

Because of the dynamic nature of the Internet, any web addresses or links contained in this book may have changed since publication and may no longer be valid. The views expressed in this work are solely those of the author and do not necessarily reflect the views of the publisher, and the publisher hereby disclaims any responsibility for them.

Any people depicted in stock imagery provided by Thinkstock are models, and such images are being used for illustrative purposes only. Certain stock imagery © Thinkstock.

ISBN: 978-1-5127-8450-3 (sc)
ISBN: 978-1-5127-8449-7 (e)

Library of Congress Control Number: 2017906445

Print information available on the last page.

WestBow Press rev. date: 6/26/2017

In loving memory and honor of my mother
Rene Mary Ann Fauntleroy
November 16, 1938–October 28, 2015

Contents

Acknowledgments and Appreciation.....................................ix

Preface...xi

Chapter 1: Be Joyful: Praise, the Joy of the Lord Is
            Our Strength...1

Chapter 2: The Word, Jesus the Worshipper,
            Freedom through the Word 7

Chapter 3: Faith: Hold On to Your Hope 16

Chapter 4: Operate in Peace: All Is Well 21

Chapter 5: Walk in Love: Victorious Living
            through the Power of Love 26

Chapter 6: Your Thought Life: Think About What
            You Are Thinking 33

Chapter 7: Looking Unto the Lord 38

Chapter 8: Prayer: Worshipping through the
            Power of Prayer 45

Chapter 9: Restoration: Is It Possible?............................54

Chapter 10: I Choose to Worship: My Choice, My
            Lifestyle 60

Chapter 11: The Redeemed Life: A Lifestyle That
            Worships God...64

Appendix 69

CONTENTS

Acknowledgments and Appreciation

My husband, Elder Nathaniel Augustusel
My children and grandchildren
My church family, Temple of Christ and
House of Prayer for All Ministries
My extended family and countless friends

Preface

Worship, or shall I say, a lifestyle of worship, develops our faith; and it takes faith to live this life, as we experience various troubles, trials, and worries. In life's journey, there will be critical times in which we will be in a position to worry. But I believe we have the authority to choose our position in life. Lately, I've decided to choose my attitude toward my stance in life. "For this is the day that the Lord has made I choose to be glad in it" (Psalm 118:24). I have discovered that I have the power of choice. I have the right to choose to be joyful, praiseworthy, kind-hearted, and forgiving each day I'm blessed to experience. I have the power to choose my attitude, my mindset, and my disposition each and every day.

What is worry, and what does it mean to worry? Basically, when you worry, you are bothered, uptight, troubled, anxious, or overly concerned about something. Worry is negative worship, or rather perverted worship that causes one to focus on something intensely; and to focus on something simply means to idolize that thing—good things as well as bad. When we pay more attention to anything other than God the Father, that thing becomes an idol. God said we should have no other gods (idols) before him (Leviticus 19:4).

Now what does it mean to worship? To worship means to bow down, honor, submit to, and recognize something or someone above oneself. I'll tell you what worship is not. It is not just going through the motions of singing spiritual songs, clapping, dancing, and holding up holy hands with your eyes closed. Worship is so much more—although that is a good part of worship, and I do enjoy being a part of it. Worship is a lifestyle that glorifies God in every way possible. Worship is living a life of trust and obedience to God as we serve him and others. The Bible tells us that our heavenly Father is looking throughout the earthly realm for true worshippers, those who will worship him in spirit and in truth (John 4:23). Many of us think that worship is just an outward expression of emotions in the form of dancing and singing. But as you read, you will discover that worship is an inward and outward expression of God's love for us and our acceptance of his love. Worship also should be the manifestation of God's peace and his Word operating in our daily lives—his forgiveness, the sharing and giving of his love, and so much more. Throughout this book, we will examine the many forms and styles in which we worship God.

Concentrating on one's troubles, problems, and becoming overly concerned about something does not glorify God. That is worry, perverted worship. Worship and worry cause someone to focus, and both can consume someone spiritually—one in a good way and one in a bad way. Are you focusing on the issues of life in a perverted way or a God-centered way? Worship causes us to focus on God and to trust him, his plans, and the purpose he has for our lives. Worry, however, takes our focus away from God and causes us not to trust him or the plans and purpose he has for us. "For I know the plans I have for you declares the Lord, plans to prosper you and not to harm you, plans to give you hope and a future" (Jeremiah 29:11). God wants us to trust him, and when we don't, that hurts him. What else is trust but exercising your faith toward God? Without faith, it is impossible to please God (Hebrews 11:6).

Throughout history and the Word, we have been reminded not to worry. Instead, we are encouraged to worship God the Father. Why should we worship instead of worry? I believe whichever position one takes—worship or worry—will usher in the presence of a spiritual force or being. This is why early in the midst of critical times—when you are tested, in pain, and in trouble—it is important to take the right position and worship God. Stop parking in a life of trouble and pain. Start worshiping God as you journey through life and as he delivers you to a better way living.

Now, if you are a believer, your position or stance should always be that of a worshiper and never that of a worrywart. When we worship instead of worry, we draw the presence, authority, and the power of God our heavenly Father into our situation. But when we worry, we invite in Satan, his presence and his power. Satan, our enemy, comes in with the spirit of fear, doubt, worry, and unbelief. Fear is to the enemy what faith is to God. Remember God did not give us a spirit of fear, but power, love, and sound minds

(2 Timothy 1:7). Jesus tells us in John 10:10 that the thief (enemy) comes to kill, steal, and destroy us, but God comes so that we might have life and have it more abundantly.

Whatever position people take during difficult times—whether as worshippers or worriers—they submit themselves and the problem to a particular spiritual force. One spiritual force will help them through worship; the other will destroy them through worry. Worshipping our heavenly Father always invites the presence of the Lord God with faith, hope, and love. But worry invites the spiritual forces of the enemy with fear, doubt, terror, dread, and destruction. No matter how bad our situation or circumstances may be, we can choose who to invite on our team. God the Father, Jesus Christ, the Holy Spirit, and you are a team. And when you have a good team that works with and supports you, you will always have favorable results and the ability to declare victory in every area of your life

When one frets, agonizes, and loses sleep because of worry, one can develop physical and even mental problems. Medical studies show that worrying causes physical illness; for example, stress can weaken the immune system, just like praise and worship can make one feel better mentally, physically, and emotionally. Worship has several other benefits:

(1) It can deny the power a particular problem has over you.
(2) It will always bring divine intervention, peace of mind, and assistance.

(3) It invites and invokes God's wisdom and direction in any situation.

There always will be benefits to worship, but there are sacrifices as well. We want the benefits that come from worshipping God, but we never want to make the sacrifices that come with it. Worship always costs you something—time, talent, emotions, resources. However, the benefits of sacrificial worship will always outweigh the sacrifices one makes. With sacrificial worship, one always experiences spiritual transformation that will improve one's well-being and divine purpose in life. Genesis 22 describes Abraham's act of sacrificial worship regarding his son. Our sacrificial worship might take place when we are in positions of uncertainty, pain, and trouble and decide to trust, love, and honor God the Father. We may not understand what in the world is going on, but we still stand on the one fact that God is faithful.

To experience benefits from worshipping God, ask yourself an important question: *what are the motives behind my worship?* Am I worshipping God because of who he is or to get something in return? Is my worship selfish and self-centered? Am I foolish enough to think that I can actually manipulate an all-knowing, all-powerful God into doing something for me that he does not want to do? It is important to realize that we were created to worship God and bring him glory on the earth in all that we say and do.

Hallelujah, Anyhow!

In Habakkuk 3:17–19 the prophet Habakkuk took the right position by worshipping and praying to God during a critical time in his life. Habakkuk gave God what I call a "yet praise," that is, praise in advance. It is praise from a deep place inside you—when there is no evidence that anything is working, but yet you know God is good and will destroy the works of the devil. For that reason, we give him pre-praise, pre-worship—praise before you see what you are hoping and believing in God for. The prophet said, "Yet I will rejoice in the Lord, I will be joyful in the God of my salvation" (Habakkuk 3:17). Habakkuk did not rejoice in the circumstances in which he found himself; he rejoiced in the fact that he had taken the right position to worship the Lord during a time of uncertainty. He could give God a yet praise, because he had heard about all the great wonders and things God had done. Habakkuk had read the testimonies of the others who had gone before him. Worshipping God the Father will lift your spirits, just as it did for the prophets of old and godly men and women of all times. Most important, it will invite the presence, power, and authority of the heavenly Father into your midst.

Chapter 1

BE JOYFUL: PRAISE, THE JOY OF THE LORD IS OUR STRENGTH

Psalms 8:2, 66:1–5, 47:1–2, 5–7
Acts 16:25–26
Romans 12:1

The Power of Praise

> About midnight Paul and Silas were praying singing hymns to God, and the other prisoners were listening to them. Suddenly there was such a violent earthquake that shook the foundation of the prison. At once all the prison doors flew open and everybody's chains came loose. (Acts 16:25)

If praying, praising, and worshipping had the power to release Paul and the others from prison, just imagine the kind of bondage from which your soul could be released. Some people may not be in a physical prison, as Paul was, but they are in a spiritual prison and are crying out for help. Often they don't even realize it, which is sad and disheartening. Not only does God inhabit our praises with supernatural power (Psalm 22:3), but prayer, praise, and worship are also liberating. Yes, God inhabits our praise. But, really, praise is more beneficial to us than it is to God.

One of the most important benefits to praising and worshipping God is that those actions will hold back the advancement of the enemy in our lives and situations. Praising and worshipping God also silences the voice of the enemy: "Out of the mouths of babes and un-weaned infants you have established strength, established, and perfected praised against your enemies, to silence the foe and the avenger" (Psalm 8:2). King David often gave himself encouragement by praising God.

I can remember a time when the only things I had to get me through a rough and trying time were praise and worship. I'd felt so downcast and troubled in my spirit. But as soon as I began to look around and thank God for the things he'd already done and those he was going to do, I was joyful, encouraged, and uplifted. Acknowledging and declaring the goodness and greatness of God encourages and liberates you. Declaring the goodness of the Lord—in your heart, out loud, and with meditation—always uplifts and encourages you, right down to the bone (1 Samuel 30:3–6). Throughout the Word, there are countless descriptions of men and women who were delivered, blessed, healed, and had their lives restored and changed for the better because of praise. These men and women of God experienced miracles simply because they chose to worship God, i.e., to declare his goodness rather than worry about their troubles and problems. They never lost sight of the fact that, no matter what happens; God the Father is good, great, and gracious unto us, his creation. This is not hard to believe, because while we were yet sinners, Christ Jesus loved us so much that he died for us so that we might have the gift of salvation, eternal life. Psalm 118:1 reminds us to "give thanks to the Lord for his mercy endues forever."

Praising God through Scriptures

> Make a joyful noise unto God, all the earth; Sing forth the honor and glory of his name; make his praise glorious! Say to God, how awesome and fearfully glorious is your work! Through the greatness of your power shall your enemies submit themselves to you with feigned and reluctant obedience all the earth shall bow down to you; they shall praise your name in song. Come and see the works of God; see how he saves his people he smites their foes; he is terrible in his doing toward the children of men. Psalm 66:1–5

> Clap your hands, all you nations; shout to God with cries of joy. For the Lord Most High is awesome, the great King over all the earth. He subdued nations under

3

us, peoples under our feet. He chose our inheritance for us, the pride of Jacob, whom he loved. God has ascended amid shouts of joy, the Lord amid the sounding of trumpets. Sing praises to God, sing praises; sing praises to our King, sing praises. For God is the King of all the earth; sing to him a psalm of praise. (Psalm 47:1–7)

A Lifestyle of Worship

I appeal to you therefore, brethren and beg of you in view of [all] the mercies of God to make a decisive dedication of your bodies [presenting all your members and faculties] as a living sacrifices, holy [devoted, consecrated] and well pleasing to God, which is your reasonable [rational, intelligent] service and spiritual worship. (Romans 12:1 AMP)

One of the most important ways to worship God is reflected in how we live in our daily lives. We should worship God in our physical bodies, in our emotions, and with our minds. Displaying Christian character and godly conduct is a form of worshipping God that glorifies him as well. Worshipping our heavenly Father should always be one's way of life, one's lifestyle. And that does not just mean to attend a service once a week and give God lip service or have an emotional experience on Sunday morning. For the

Word says that we ought to be living epistles ready to be read by all people; 2 Corinthians 10:13 reminds us that the only scripture some people will ever read is to observe the Christian lives of others living around them in this world. Be mindful of how you live and worship, because you never know who is reading your life and trying to decide whether to give his or her life to Christ. For we have come to know that a lifestyle of worship is so much more than just singing songs, dancing, and moving around.

Praising God is a major part of worshipping God. There are seven specific expressions of praise in the Bible. When we see the word *praise*, it could be a reference to one of seven Hebrew words (pronunciations in parentheses):

Seven Types of Praise

1. *Yadah* (yaw-*daw*) means to worship or praise God with extended hands, to show reverence and adoration toward God with lifted hands. (Psalms 9:1, 28:7, 33:2, 42:5; 2 Chronicles 7)
2. *Towdah* (to-*daw*) means to extend one's right hand to indicate agreement about what will be done, although it has not happened yet. All at once with extended hands sacrificially praising, thanking, and being in agreement with him. (Psalms 22:3, 33:1, 50:23)
3. *Barak* (baw-*rak*) means to kneel down, to bow down low, as a sign of adoration and reverence. To give reverence to God by humbling oneself before him, blessing, saluting, and praising him. (Psalms 95:6, 103)

5

4. *Tehillah* (tel-hil-*law*) means to sing spontaneously from the heart; to give unrehearsed and unprepared praise directly to God. (Psalms 22:3, 33:1, 34:1, 40:3, 66:2; 2; Chronicles 20:22)

5. *Zamar* (zaw-*mar*) is the most common form of praise, and it means to praise God in music or song, to worship with instruments. It means to pluck the strings, to play a musical instrument. (Psalms 92:1, 150)

6. *Halal* (haw-*lal*) is known as the most fun form of praise, because it requires worshippers to step outside of themselves and their dignity for a moment. It means to be clamorously foolish, to boast or shine. *Halal* is the origin of the word *hallelujah*, which means "praise the Lord." (1 Chronicles 16:4, Nehemiah 12:24)

7. *Shabach* (shaw-*bakh*) means to proclaim with a loud voice and to praise in a loud tone, unashamed and uninhibited with an attitude of freedom or accomplishment. This type of praise is more than just a loud shout; it's the idea of putting your whole being into your praise. (Psalm 63:3–4)

Chapter 2

THE WORD, JESUS THE WORSHIPPER, FREEDOM THROUGH THE WORD

Jeremiah 1:12

John 1:14, 8:32, 10:16, 14:9

Psalms 23, 107:20, 115–118, 119:50

Romans 8:3, 10:17, 15:4

2 Timothy 3:16–17

Mark 4:14–20

Proverbs 4:20–22

Matthew 1:23, 8:5–13, 15:18–19

Luke 1:37–38, 22–39–46

Hebrew 4:12–15, 12:2

Isaiah 55:11

Galatians 2:28, 3:20

Philippians 2:5–11

Colossians 1:19, 2:9, 3:1

James 1:21

2 Corinthians 3:2–-3
Jude 1:20

> "My son, give attention to my words;
> Incline your ear to my sayings.
>
> Do not let them depart from your sight,
> keep them in the midst of your heart;
> For they are life to those who find
> them and health to one's whole body."
> (Proverbs 4:20–22)

Who does not want to be free from trouble, problems, and worries? Who wants to be consumed by worry and trouble? We can have troubles, but they don't have to consume us. Jesus said that if you abide in him and hold to his teachings, then you are his disciples—and his disciples will know the truth (God's Word), and the truth will set them free (John 8:32). Do you desire to be set free of something? I'm sure the answer is yes. Then it is imperative that you continue to learn and know the Word of God, and set yourself free. Here, the term *know* means to accept and then continue. What Jesus is saying we should accept God's truth and continue. Countless events in the Bible and in the lives of folk who worship God through the Word—the truth—reveal that people were set free in the midst of trouble, sin, and destruction. Jesus said that in this life we will have trouble, but he told us to be encouraged, to continue in the truth, and to stay focused. He promised us that we shall overcome.

We live in a fallen world and problems and troubles will come. But just as Jesus overcame, we too shall have to victory and overcome. Jesus stayed focused in the midst of every troubling situation and circumstance, and we should learn from his example. The truth of God's Word will produce a blessed life. Those of us who desire a blessed life, are seeking to be free of troubles, or are engaged in spiritual warfare need to build up our faith. Hebrews 12:2 says we should "look to Jesus who is the author and finisher of our faith." The Word of God also tells us that "faith comes by hearing and hearing the word" (Romans 10:17). We will be built up in faith only when we know, meditate, and speak the Word of God when dealing with trouble, fears, problems and concerns, instead of panicking and giving in. By doing this we are saying several things: First, we are telling God that we honor, love, and trust in him and his Word. Second, we are training our minds and spirits to agree with what God has said about us, instead of listening to what the enemy tries to dictate to us. When we engage in worship during trying times, we are training our spirits to be at peace, the God kind of peace that passes all understanding. One can experience this type of peace by staying focused on the Lord. This peace also evokes God's presence. We have the power of God on our side, because the Lord said that he would watch over his Word to perform it (Jeremiah 1:12). God is watching over you to see if you honor his Word so he can perform it.

We worship and honor God by knowing, studying, speaking, understanding, and believing in his Word. He honors his Word above everything else. To honor God's

Word is to honor him, and that's worship. Jesus said that he was the Word that became flesh and dwelt among us (John 1:14). God said that he sent forth his Word and healed the children of Israel, rescuing them from the grave. If God and his Word did that for the children of Israel, his Word, issued from our mouths, will do the same for us. For God's Word is alive and active (Hebrews 4:12). Throughout the Bible, we are reassured about the benefits of trusting in God and his Word:

> This is my comfort and consolation in my affliction that your Word has revived me and given me life. (Psalm 119:50)

> Whatever things were written in earlier times was written for our learning and instruction, so that we through the perseverance, the encouragement and comfort of the scripture that we might have hope. (Romans 15:4)

> Every scripture is God-breathed (given by his inspiration) and profitable for instruction, for reproof and conviction of sin, for correction of error and discipline in obedience, (and) for training in righteousness (in holy living, in conformity to God's will in complete and proficient, well fitted and thoroughly equipped for every good work. (2 Timothy 3:16–17)

Sowing the word of God in your heart will produce a blessed life. I'm not saying that you won't have challenges simply by reading and knowing God's Word. However, I do believe you will have fewer troubles and problems. The enemy of our souls can't just say anything to our minds and hearts. We can live a victorious life and overcome the challenges we face because of God's Word: "therefore get rid of all moral filth and the evil that is so prevalent and humbly accept the word planted in you, which can save you" (James 1:21). The word *save* is a reference to salvation, which originates from a Greek term, *soteria*, meaning rescue, deliverance, escape, recovery, wellness, and prosperity. In other words, if you allow God's Word to be planted within you, it will deliver you from a life of destruction. You will escape much—though not all—of life's troubles; even when faced with trouble, you can live a blessed life. When the Word of God is planted or sown in your heart and transforms your mind, you will live a blessed life. We plant the Word in us when we read it, pray it, hear it, listen to it, speak it, and simply meditate upon it as much as possible. Amen!

The book of Mark (4:14–20) includes this allegory:

> The farmer sows the word. Some people are like seed along the path, where the word is sown. As soon as they hear the word, Satan comes right away to take away the word sown in them. Others are like seed sown on rocky places: they hear the word and at once receive it with joy. But since

they have no root [they are not rooted or grounded in the Word] they last only a short time. When trouble or persecution comes because of the word, they quickly fall away. Still others, like seed sown among thorns, they hear the word, and the desires for other things come in and choke the word making it unfruitful. Others like seed sown on good soil, they hear the word, accept it and produce a crop—thirty, sixty, or even a hundred times what was sown. (Mark 4:14–20)

You see, sometimes because of the Word, you will have troubles, but that is the enemy trying to distract you and stop you from prospering and walking in victory. Ask yourself this question: have I allowed God's Word to produce a blessed life through me? Let God's Word produce blessings through you. Remember, Jesus himself said that we would have troubles in this life, but be encouraged. He overcame the troubles of life and so can we, because of his power, his love and his Word. By planting the Word in our hearts, minds, and spirits, we train ourselves to be more like God. For our spiritual development, we should learn to saturate ourselves with God's Word. We need to nurture and feed our spirits with the Word so that we can become stronger spiritually and strengthen our faith. Whenever we feed and nurture something, it will grow and become strong. Once your faith is strong, you can speak the Word of God in faith and tackle any problems, troubles, or fears that stand in the way of a better life.

Speaking the Word of God is also known as worship. Worshipping God through the Word—by speaking, reading, or meditating upon it—is a spiritual exercise we cannot ignore if we are going to be strengthened in our faith. In the midst of troubles and problems, we need strong faith. Not only do we become strong in faith, we strengthen others as well. We need to continuously plant the Word of God in our hearts, because out of our hearts flow the concerns of life (Proverbs 4:23, Matthew 15:18–19).

Matthew 8:5–13 includes an excellent account of the power of the spoken Word. This scripture describes a centurion, a person of great faith, who believed in the power of God's words. He knew the power of speaking the Word of God in faith. When his servant was paralyzed and sick, near death, he went to Jesus in the town of Capernaum and asked him to heal his servant. As Jesus was getting ready to return to the man's home with him and heal his servant, the centurion said Jesus did not need to go with him, but just send forth his word and heal him. In Matthew 8:8, the centurion says, "Lord, I do not deserve to have you come under my roof. But just say the word, and my servant will be healed." Jesus told the man to go, and it would be done for him, because of his faith in the Lord and his words. God honored this man's great faith in the spoken word, and in that very moment the man's servant was healed.

Isaiah 55:11 also reminds us about the power of the spoken Word. God said that his Word goes forth out of his mouth and shall not return to him void, without producing any effect but it shall accomplish that which God pleased, purposed, prospered and sent the Word to do. Now it is awesome and reassuring to know that God the Father is that faithful. But the most amazing thing about speaking God's Word is that it is so mighty and powerful that if it is spoken by anyone, it still has the same anointing power and the power to produce.

Jesus the Word, the Worshipper

Although we know Jesus worshipped through prayer and by ministering the Word of his Father, we hardly talk about Jesus as a worshipper through songs and hymns. The Bible encourages us to sing hymns and songs of praise. We know Jesus as a prayer warrior, a healer, and a miracle worker. But many of us never talk about him as one who thanked and glorified God the Father constantly by singing the Psalms. No matter what, Jesus was a worshipper. When he faced trouble or uncertainty, he never stopped worshipping his Father in every way imaginable. Even before he was crucified he went into deep prayer offering all of himself to God the Father (Luke 22:39–46). We must know that it was a part of Jesus culture and tradition to worship in song and hymns, particularly during the Passover celebration. Psalms, such as Psalms 115 to 118 were sung at the end of the Passover celebration, and were very much a part of Jesus upbringing.

The Word took on human form and came to dwell among us. The Greek terms for *Word* are *Rhema* and *Logos*. *Rhema* means spoken word. When Gabriel, the angel of the Lord, told Mary about the child she would conceive, Mary's response was "Let it be according to thy word" (Luke 1:37–38). *Logos* means the Divine Word, the second person of the Trinity, incarnate in the person of Jesus (1 John 1:1–14). God is a spirit, who sends a message of truth. God's Word became flesh, took on human form, and dwelt among us. God became flesh so he could be our high priest, able to empathize with our weaknesses and to be tempted in every way, just like we are. But the Word, i.e., Jesus, did not sin. Jesus was the Word that became flesh and dwelt among us, so we could become living epistles, the living Word, and dwell among people (John 1:14). The scriptures tell us in 2 Corinthians 3:2 that we are letter-written—not with pen and ink, but with the Spirit of the living God.

Chapter 3

FAITH: HOLD ON
TO YOUR HOPE

Ecclesiastes 9:4
2 Corinthians 5:7
Romans 4:17–25, 10:11, 17, 15:13
Hebrews 10:23, 38–39, 11:6
James 1:6–8

"Let us hold fast to the profession of our faith without wavering; for he is faithful that promised" (Hebrews 11:6).

Having faith in God, in the Word of God, and in his ability to keep his promises is a form of worship. What is faith? According to the book of Hebrews, faith is the assurance, the confirmation, the title deed of the things we hope for, the proof of things we do not see and the conviction of this reality. Faith perceives as real what is not revealed to the senses. In other words, faith is holding on to the hope of obtaining something you have not seen but desire to possess. Worship, in its greatest form, is holding on to your faith and hope in the face of trials, struggles, and adverse conditions. Now this is worship, because what you are choosing to do is to trust God instead of giving into the various issues you face in life. God is glorified when we choose to trust him, exercise our faith, and hold on to hope. Anytime God is glorified, it is considered worship. When we glorify or worship God, we reveal his faithfulness and power. However, when we draw back, or operate in fear, doubt, and unbelief, God does not get the glory, and his power and faithfulness do not show (Romans 4:18–25).

Against all hope, Father Abraham believed and became the father of many nations without weakening, wavering, or staggering in his faith regarding God's promises. Abraham was fully persuaded in the midst of trials and struggles that God had the power to do what he'd promised. The "Father of Faith" faced his fear, his issues, and the fact that his body was as good as dead—and that his wife Sarah's womb was too old to produce the promised child. But he held on to his faith, and he didn't waver. Abraham worshipped God in faith, and it was credited to him as righteousness. When Abraham had nothing else to hold on to, he held on to his faith and hope for two reasons: First, he was wise enough to understand that as long as there was life in his body, there was hope that God would do what he had promised. "Anyone among the living has hope. A live dog is better than a dead lion" (Ecclesiastes 9:4). Second, no man who ever believed in, trusted in, and relied on God was ever humiliated, embarrassed, shamed, or disappointed.

Some people are afraid to trusting what they can't see, but believing and taking God at his word is a form of worship in its purest form. Just believe (Romans 10:11). In Sunday school, we used to sing a little song: "Only believe. All things are possible if you only believe." Jesus told Martha and Mary to believe when he called their brother Lazarus out of the grave (John 11:38–43). As Jesus healed and delivered people, he would tell them not to doubt, but only believe. When the daughter of Jairus, a synagogue leader, was close to death, Jesus told him that the child was asleep and not dead. Jesus said, "Just believe." Jairus's neighbors laughed and mocked him, but he believed Jesus, and his daughter was healed. Sometimes in the face of discouragement and disappointment, the only thing you have is the belief that God the Father can and will turn things around. Now that type of belief in God is worship.

"For we walk by faith, we regulate our lives and conduct ourselves by our conviction or beliefs in our relationship to God and divines things with trust and a holy fervor" (2 Corinthians 5:7). Since we should walk by faith, God the Father put a measure of his faith in all of his children. But it is our responsibility to develop the faith that he put in us. Faith is matured or developed by the Word of God only; that is why we must continuously keep the Word before us. As we discussed in a previous chapter, one of the best ways to get rid of trouble and worry is to worship God through the Word. Meditating upon the Word as much as possible is worship. Faith only comes by hearing and hearing God's Word (Romans 10:17). Hearing and hearing the Word over and over again is worship that not only will strengthen your faith, it will allow you to grow spiritually and give God glory in your Christian walk. We should not waiver in our faith, because as we develop it, we will be greatly rewarded. Through double-mindedness, we waiver in our faith, and God does not honor unbelief. Without faith, it is impossible to honor and please God. The Word tells us that whoever comes to God must believe that he exists and that he is a reward to those who earnestly seek him (Hebrews 11:6). Since God does not honor or reward unbelief and double-mindedness, we must examine ourselves, and make sure we are not operating in unbelief. When you waiver in your faith, one minute you believe and trust God, and in the next, you operate in doubt, wondering if God will ever come through for you. God said that anyone who is double-minded is unstable in all of his or her ways and should not expect anything from him (James 1:6–8). If we stand and hold fast in our faith during difficult times, we will see the salvation of the Lord, his deliverance, and his help will come through mightily for us in all of his glory. Romans 15:13 tells us that the God of hope fills us with all joy and peace as we trust in him, so that we may overflow with hope by the power of the Holy Spirit. As one reads his powerful and loving words, we can't help but know that as we trust in God, we will not be disappointed. Trusting in God is to worship him.

Doubt and unbelief have an element of fear in them. God did not give people a spirit of fear (2 Timothy 1:7). Fear is accompanied by torment, but God's perfect love casts fear out of us if we receive it (1 John 4:18). Since God did not give us fear, when it comes, we must not accept it. God takes no pleasure in those who do not operate in faith and give into fear without hope. Fear is perverted faith that does not glorify God. What faith is to God, fear is to Satan. Our faith will invite the power of God into our circumstances and situations, but the spirit of fear opens us up to Satan and invites him into our lives. God is pleased when we exercise our faith. However, Satan is glad when we walk in fear instead. "Without faith, it is impossible to please God," Hebrews 11:6. We are reminded in Hebrews 10:38–39, that if we hold back our faith, we will be destroyed, because fear gives Satan power and permission to operate in our midst. God says that his righteous ones will always live by faith, and if they shrink back, he will not be pleased. If they believe, they will be saved, but if they hold back, they will be destroyed. In other words, those who trust God the Father and walk in faith will be delivered and made whole in every way. Going forth in our faith and not holding back on God is a way of worshipping him.

Chapter 4

OPERATE IN PEACE: ALL IS WELL

2 Kings 4:8–36
John 16:32–33
Colossians 3:15
Philippians 4:6–7
Isaiah 26:3
1 Peter 3:11

"Let the peace of Christ rule in your heart, since as members of one body you were called to peace" (Colossians 3:15.) I love this scripture because it tells me to let the peace of Christ have its power in my heart. It also says that we have a choice: keep the peace of God, or focus on problems and trouble. In the midst of trying times, one must learn the spiritual discipline of operating in peace. It is possible to operate in peace when chaos is all around you, but for some it can be very hard. Keeping a clear head, maintaining calm emotions, and walking in peace during trying times is beneficial. Practicing the discipline of operating in peace is vital to one's spiritual development simply because it demonstrates that you trust God (Isaiah 26:3). God will keep you in perfect peace if your mind is set, stays on him, and is steadfast in your thinking about him and his goodness. Operating in peace is a form of worshipping God, experiencing his very presence within you.

Our heart and minds are protected when we trust God and operate in peace. We must protect our hearts and minds, because life flows from them. Sometimes we experience adversity, sent by the enemy, that's designed to destroy us. In those trying times we must protect our hearts and emotions, so that our problems don't have power over us. Purposely walking in peace during adverse times will keep you from operating in anger, bitterness, and retaliation. Believe it or not, the presence of God can be invited into any situation in which you practice the spiritual discipline of operating peace. We worship God through the practice of peace. Peace has the power and evidence of God's love and presence. And wherever God's love and presence are, there will always be victory. This is why Jesus said, "My peace I give to you and leave with you and nothing and no one can take it away from you," John 14:27 Now, no one can take God's peace from you, but you can give it up or give it away. The choice of whether to keep God's peace is yours. Hold on to the peace God gave you, and don't allow anything or anyone to steal it; as a matter of fact, go after it. First Peter 3:11 tells us to seek peace and pursue it. In other words, seek God as you pursue him by worshipping him through the peace he has given you.

Jesus told his disciples that troubling times were coming and that they would feel as if they were alone in the world. However, he reassured them that they would never be alone. In the midst of trouble, you may feel alone, but God the Father promises to be with you. Have you ever felt isolated when facing problems and trouble? Jesus told the disciples not to worry, to have courage and be confident, for he has overcome the world and its troubles due to perfect peace. The term *perfect* here means mature. Jesus had mature peace; he remained calm during horrible times, and so can we. Jesus had mature peace for two reasons: (1) he recognized and understood that the peace he possessed came from God the Father, and he had a choice to keep it; (2) Jesus also trusted and had confidence in God's peace; he knew that the peace he possessed had been tested, tried, and proven to have power to bring him through any trial or troubles he would ever face (John 16:32–33).

It Is Well with My Soul

Second Kings 4:26–36 describes a Shunammite woman who had lost her son after years of wanting one. The moment her son died, she refused to be shaken and rattled in her spirit. She refused to surrender her peace to problems, fear, or evil thoughts. In other words, she did not look for and expect something bad to happen (Proverbs 15:15). That is called worry, and worrying is not of God. At once, she gathered her things together and went to see Elisha, the man of God who had prophesied that she and her aged husband would have the child they wanted so desperately. Although this Shunammite woman was facing a tragedy, the sudden death of her son, her faith was not shaken. And because she held on to her hope, operated in peace, and kept her emotions calm, her son's life was restored.

I love how this woman responded to Gehazi, Elisha's assistant, when he went to meet her and see what was wrong. She said, "It is well." She did not blab all her business to anybody and everybody, like a lot of folk do. Nor did she panic and allow the spirit of fear to rob her of her trust and faith in God. She had blessed assurance; she kept her composure together under pressure. She held on to her peace until she could talk with the man of God who had told her that she would have a child. "It is well," she said, because she knew that she could trust a God who had given her a child of promise. Elisha told Gehazi to run and say to her, "It is well with you? Well with your husband? Well with your child?"(2 Kings 4:26) She answered, "It is well," even though it was not. She spoke those things that were not as if they were (Romans 4:17). She had enough faith to speak about things that had not happened yet. The peace the Shunammite woman possessed helped her to speak words of faith regarding her situation and troubles.

That is just what you and I should do. Don't worry, and go off in doubt and unbelief. Possess the very peace of God, and speak words of faith when in troubling situations. It is important to understand that life and death are in the power of the tongue (Proverbs 18:21). As the peace of God leads you, no matter what you come up against, continue to speak God's words, and let his peace reside within you. When we remember to live in God's peace and speak his

Word, his promises, his purpose, and his plans will come to pass as we remain in peace with the power of his Word. No matter what comes your way, refuse to give up, and let peace rule in your heart.

> And God's peace shall be yours, that tranquil state of a soul assured of its salvation through Christ and so fearing nothing from God and being content with its earthly lot of whatever sort that is, that peace which transcends all understanding shall garrison and mount guard over your heart and minds in Christ Jesus. (Philippians 4:7 AMP)

Chapter 5

WALK IN LOVE: VICTORIOUS LIVING THROUGH THE POWER OF LOVE

Isaiah 48:17
Romans 5:5, 8:28–39, 12:9–12, 13:8–14
1 Corinthians 8:1–3, 13:1–8
Ephesians 3:16–19
1 John 4:18

Walking in God's love is another form of worship. What is love? The Bible says that love is a spirit and God is a spirit and that he is also love (1 John 4:8). That would make love alive and an active spiritual force. And where there is love, the power and presence of Almighty God is there. 1 Corinthians 13:1–8 is known as the love chapter:

> Love endures suffering long and is patient and kind; love never is envious nor boils over with jealousy, it is not

boastful or vainglorious, does not display itself haughtily. It is not conceited [arrogant and inflated with pride]; it is not rude [unmannerly] and does not act unbecomingly. Love [God's love in us] does not insist on its own rights or its own way, for it is not self-seeking; it is not touchy or fretful or resentful; it takes no account of the evil done to it [it pays no attention to a suffered wrong]. It does not rejoice at injustice and unrighteousness but rejoices when right and truth prevail. Love bears up under anything that comes and is ever ready to believe the best of every person, its hopes are fadeless under all circumstances and it endures everything without weakening. Love never fails never fades out or become obsolete or comes to an end.

When we practice love, we are actually practicing God's presence within us. Our love walk is an important part of our Christian walk and spiritual growth and development, because if we allow it to, God's love will transform us. I believe the more we yield to the spirit of love, the more we walk in the power of God. As we walk in God's power, his unfailing love in our lives will turn things around completely for the better. Love will always affect your quality of life. We must realize that we need help from God the Father. We should also ask him to teach us how to live and walk in love his way. Our heavenly Father can teach us how to overcome any trouble through the power of his love.

The Word says that God's love will never fail, and I know this to be true, because his love is the foundation and source of all things that are good in our lives. Our faith will not work without love. We need to allow the love of the Father to operate in us for our faith to work. Therefore, we should never invite the spirit fear of into a situation by thinking that God's love will not work on our behalf. Understand that perfect love casts out fear (1 John 4:18). Without love, God the Father does not hear or answer our prayers. Why; because God is love. God's love will always bring us into his presence, his peace, his power and prosperity. Wherever the presence of God is, there is victory. When we face trouble, problems, and adversity, we should not spend time worrying and fearing. Instead, we need to worship in the assurance of God's love. Wherever God's love is, his presence will be, and his presence will always guide us in the way we should go. "I'm the Lord your Redeemer, the Holy One of Israel; I am the Lord your God, who teaches you to profit'" (Isaiah 48:17). God loves us so much, he redeemed us. In other words, he took us from a life of destruction, death, and damnation to a land of a better life that shows us how to prosper (John 10:10). When we did not deserve anything but death, God redeemed us anyway, by exchanging his Son's life for ours. Jesus went through destruction and death for us, so that we could live and have life more abundantly. Now, that's true love.

We can walk in love; we have the ability to do so, because God has poured his love into our hearts. However, we must receive it, accept it, and operate in it (Romans 5:5). Since God has poured his love in our hearts, we can operate in love toward God, others, and, yes, even ourselves. A person operating in love is someone who is courageous and has self-control. Being able to walk in love causes a person to be secure and to hold his or her peace in the midst of adversity, confusion, and trouble. Christian love is one of the highest forms of spiritual warfare. God's love is spiritual warfare that will empower you and defeat the enemy. This is why God commands and reminds us to walk in his love.

> I pray that out of his glorious riches that he may strengthen you with power through his spirit in your inner being. So that Christ may dwell in your hearts through faith. And I pray that you, being rooted and established in love, may have power, together with all the saints, to grasp flow wide and long and high and deep is the love of Christ, and to know this love surpasses knowledge—that you may be filled to the measure of all the fullness of God. (Ephesians 3:16–19)

When we decide to walk in love, regardless of our troubles and the pressing issues in life, we are worshipping God, and we will experience the power of victorious living.

Living victoriously over the issues of life, I believe, is a choice—one that glorifies God. Whenever we glorify God, we are actually worshipping him. It is our choice to believe several things that the Word of God tells us about his love for us. First, it is our choice whether or not to believe that God has poured out his love, i.e., his power, into our hearts. Second, the Bible tells us that God is not a man who lies or repents from the promises he has made to us (Numbers 23:19). Finally, the Word of God tells us that we can be assured that all things—good, bad, or indifferent—will work together for the good of those who love God and are called according to his purpose (Romans 8:29). No matter how we look at it, the power of God's love is working for us, whether or not we realize it. If we really stopped to understand the magnitude of God's love for us, we would worship the Father at all times. We would worship with the assurance of the spirit of love, rather than worry when we face adverse times.

> Who shall separate us from the love of Christ? Shall trouble or hardship or persecution or famine or nakedness or danger or sword? As it is written, "for your sake we face death all day long; we are considered as sheep to be slaughtered." No, in all these things we are more than conquerors though him who loved us. For I am convinced that neither death nor life, neither angels nor demons, neither height nor depth, nor anything else in all creation,

will be able to separate us from the love
of God that is in Christ Jesus our Lord.
(Romans 8:35–39)

After reading and meditating this passage from
Romans, you can't help but believe that you can make it
through anything and everything with God's love.

Love for God the Father, love for thy neighbor, and
love for oneself will empower one to live the victorious and
abundant life that Jesus promised us. No one who operates
in the spirit of love can deny its power. God gave us the
power of love to live a blessed life. Reflect on the power of
love through the Word of God, which tells us that our love
must be sincere.

> Hate what is evil; cling to what is good.
> Be devoted to one another in brotherly
> love. Honor one another above yourselves.
> Never be lacking in zeal, but keep your
> spiritual fervor, serving the Lord. Be joyful
> in hope, patient in affliction and faithful in
> prayer. Share with God's people who are
> in need. Practice hospitality. Bless those
> who persecute you; bless and do not curse.
> Rejoice with those who rejoice; mourn
> with those who mourn. Live in harmony
> with one another. Do not be proud, but
> be willing to associate with people of low
> position. Do not be conceited. Do not
> repay anyone evil for evil. Be careful to do

what is right in the eyes of everybody. If it is possible, as far as it depend on you, live at peace with everyone. Do not take revenge, my friends, but leave room for God's wrath, for it is written: it is mine to avenge; I will repay, says the Lord. One the contrary: if your enemy is hungry, feed him; if he is thirst, give him something to drink. In doing this, you will heap burning coals on his head. Do not be overcome by evil, but overcome evil with good. (Romans 12:9–21)

Chapter 6

YOUR THOUGHT LIFE: THINK ABOUT WHAT YOU ARE THINKING

Luke 10:27, 16:13
Romans 8:5-8, 12:1–2
Philippians 2:5, 4:8
2 Corinthians 2:16, 4:4, 10:5
Isaiah 26:3
Colossians 3:16
Proverbs 4:23, 47
Acts 17:11

People who submit to their earthly natures, the flesh, are controlled by ungodly desires. They set their minds on that which pleases, satisfies, and gratifies the flesh. However, those who submit to the Spirit of God are controlled by the desires of the Holy Spirit, and their minds seek out things that gratify God (Romans 8:5–8).

We need to control our thoughts if we are going to be

victorious in the battle against our worries, troubles, and problems. How did Jesus manage to achieve victory in every area of his life, even his thought life? I believe he had power, authority, and victory in every area of life because he possessed the mind of God. He allowed God's mindset to operate within him. That is why the scriptures tell us to let the mindset that was in Christ Jesus be inside of us as well.

One day I received a revelation. The scripture asked, *Will you allow the mind of Christ to be in you?* Be in harmony with the mind of Christ. Will *you* allow the mind of Christ to be in you? When we have a double mindset, we are in a state of confusion, and the peace of God cannot reside within us. The scripture tells us that you cannot serve two masters at the same time, because you will love one and hate the other. Similarly, you cannot have two mindsets at the same time; you will go forth with one mindset, and leave the other behind. You can't move forward and backward at the same time.

You can obtain the mind of God by meditating, studying, and knowing the Word of God for yourself. Philippians 2:5 more or less asks you to let this mind be inside you. In other words, this scripture asks if you will allow God's mind to be in you freely, without doubt, restriction, and hesitation. God gave you free will to choose what to do with your life, including your mind. For instance, if you want peace during troubled times, Isaiah 26:3 says, "Thou will keep him in perfect peace whose mind is stayed on thee." When you worship God with your mind, his perfect peace will minister to you at critical times. Worshipping God with your mind means purposely choosing your thoughts and filling your mind with God's Word. If you want to have the mind of Christ within you, pursue it, and you can have it.

Because God gave us free will to decide whether or not to worship him, worshipping him with our minds is our responsibility. Taking an active role in having the right and spiritual mindset is also our responsibility. In the mind, we create, imagine, and perceive. In the mind, we come to know a thing and begin to understand it. Everything begins and ends with a thought. Every action and reaction, creation and all existence, began with a thought. This is why we need to keep a positive mindset and constantly be aware of what we are thinking. Studies have shown that negative thoughts can cause physical illness and release harmful chemicals into the body. All of us move from a carnal life into a spirit-filled life once we receive the free gift of salvation and are transformed in the spirit of our minds (Romans 12:2). When our minds are changed, our actions and reactions will change; then our lives will change. It's that simple. We will deal with our troubles and problems differently and experience victory more often if we worship God with our minds. However, we will never see any change in our lives if we do not allow the Word of God to transform our minds. Your life will change for the better if you worship God with your mind.

It is in our minds that we first experience spiritual warfare. The enemy knows that if our thought life is in bondage, we will not give glory to God. We were created to worship God with our whole beings, including our minds. "You shall love the Lord our God with all your heart and with all your soul and with all your strength and with your entire mind" (Luke 10:27). Second Corinthians 10:5 tells us to fight for our minds by casting out all opinions that go against the knowledge of God and making every thought obedient to Christ. We have the authority and power to control our thoughts. The enemy will use anything and everything to attack our minds with negative and destructive ideas. Now if we know and operate in the power and the authority of God through the blood of Christ, the Word of God, and our thought life, we will achieve victory throughout our lives. If we want to know how to worship God in our thought life, we must first learn the Word. Know and accept the Word; think and meditate on the Word of God in good times and in the midst of adversity.

People are three-part beings. First, we are spiritual beings who connect with our heavenly Father, who is a spirit. God the Father lives in us, through us, and with us. As we live for him in this world, he propels us from the life we live in the earthly realm.

Second, we possess a soul. The soul is where our emotions live; where we feel, think and want. It is where we experience life as the spiritual beings we need to be to equip our souls to battle through life successfully. It is God's desire that we live a beautiful life by worshipping him and giving him glory in our daily walks with him. Instead of giving in to the negativity and destructiveness in this fallen world, we have within us the power of God, which allows us to live victoriously and overcome anything. We are redeemed people living in a fallen world. Life will come at us with all kinds of fears, hurt, and pain, with spirits of aggravation, frustration, intimidation, and manipulation.

The enemy of this world has blinded people's minds so they cannot see the goodness of God. The enemy only wants us to see him coming at us with all sorts of the aforementioned distractions, issues, and drama (2 Corinthians 4:4). We have to cast down the negative spirits, suggestions, and ideas that try to invade our thought lives, our minds. You purposely have to take off the old man, your old self and be transformed and renewed in the spirit of your mind (Roman 12:1-2). And then let the mind of Christ be in you, dwell in your daily (Philippians 2:5, Colossians 3:16).

Third, each person's physical being is his or her mind and heart, which have two different functions. The mind in the natural, physical realm has the function and ability to think, understand, comprehend, and perceive. The heart in its natural function helps regulate the flow of blood throughout the body. However, I believe that in the spiritual realm, the mind and the heart are one and the same. In Proverb 4:7, the heart is understood as operating as a mind: "as a man think in his heart of himself so is he, now that's our thought life." Proverbs 4:23 instructs us to guard our hearts and our mindsets, because out of them flow the issues of life. The word of God is helpful for our mind set and our thought life; as we understanding life to be; and as we conduct ourselves accordingly. The Word of God reminds and instructs us how we should think and to have a godly mind set. Philippians 4:8 says it best when it tells us to: "Finally brethren whatsoever things are true, whatsoever things are honest, whatsoever things are just, whatsoever things are of good report, if there be any virtue, and if there be any praise think on these things."

Chapter 7

LOOKING UNTO THE LORD

Deuteronomy 28
Matthew 4:8–10
Isaiah 1:19–20, 48:17
Psalm 121
Proverbs 3:5–6
Ephesians 4:18
Hebrews 12:1–2, 13:5–6 (AMP)
1 Corinthians 10:13
1 Peter 1:1–8 (AMP)
Colossians 1:13
Philippians 4:6

> Again, the devil took him to a very high mountain and showed him kingdoms of the world and their splendor. "All this I will give you," he said, "if you will bow down and worship me." Jesus said to him, "Away from me, Satan! For it is written: Worship

the Lord your God and serve him only."
(Matthew 4:8–10)

Focusing on anything can be a form of worship. Life's problems can consume you and turn into perverted worship. Nothing in this life should take one's focus away from God the Father, his love for us and his power. When faced with life's problems and struggles, it is always good to do what you can do, what you need to do, and what you've got to do; after that, leave the rest in the hands of the Lord. You may ask yourself, *What do I need to do in this situation?* Well, prayer is always a good place to start. Remember the little song we sang in Sunday school: "Just a little talk with Jesus will make everything all right." Believe me when I say we can talk to God the Father about any and everything. "Do not be anxious about anything, but in everything, by prayer and petition, with thanksgiving, present your requests to God" (Philippians 4:6). There is nothing in this world too big or too small to talk to our heavenly Father about. As a matter of fact, prayer is one of the ways in which we look to God for answers, direction, and hope during difficult times. Not only can we look to God through the vehicle of prayer, we can also read and meditate on his Word. Looking to the Lord through his Word is life-giving, life-changing, and rewarding. At the end of this chapter I've listed some scripture passages that will help you journey through life's difficulties and stay focused on worshipping God. Read them, pray them, say them, sing them, and meditate on them as much as possible, and watch the Word transform your life.

Unfortunately, trouble can enter our lives for any number of reasons. Sometimes, trouble occurs because we have opened the door to some demonic activity. Some trouble comes because we have *willfully ignored* God and his Word. Willful ignorance means we purposefully choose not to know or do something. Some people have hard hearts toward God and the things of God; they choose not to know him or anything about him. God gave us the power of choice and free will. Although God created us, what we do with that will is our decision. He gave us the power to exercise our free will. "They are darkened in their understanding and separated from the life of God because of the ignorance that is in them due to the hardening of their hearts" (Ephesians 4:18). Whenever one is separated from a life of knowing God, who created everything and knows all things, one will have a world of trouble and problems. Without a sense of direction, that person will be lost.

Sin, rebellion, and disobedience also open the door to trouble, disaster, and demonic activity. Look at what Isaiah 1:19–20 says: "If you are willing and obedient, you will eat the fat of the land, but if you refuse and rebel, you shall be devoured." In other words, prosperity will come into your life if you are obedient to God and live a godly lifestyle. Deuteronomy 28 includes a whole list of curses that arise from a life of sin and rebellion and a list of blessings that arise from a life of obedience. We must realize that whatever we decide to do with our lives, there will be consequences depending on whether we choose to operate in obedience or disobedience to God. Based on this truth, we have the power to keep a lot of problems away from our lives or to open the door and welcome them in. Remember, God gave us free will; he will not impose his will on us, but his will is best. The choice is ours—blessings or curses. What will you do with the power of your choice?

There will be times when the enemy will attack us, simply because we are the children of God, and the devil does not like God's children. It is the devil's job to stop God's people from reaching their divine destiny. But our heavenly Father has delivered us from the control and dominion of darkness and transferred us into the kingdom of his Son (Colossians 1:13 AMP). God has delivered us out of the hand of darkness.

However, there are several things we must know, without a shadow of doubt: First, we must know who God is and who he says he is. Second, we must know about God's love for us. Third, we must know who we are and who we are in him. *I'm the righteousness of God in Christ Jesus—not because of anyone else or anything I've done, but because of who Jesus is. I'm the head and not the tail. I'm a new creation in Christ Jesus.* These statements of faith are facts and are found in the Word of God. We have to know and accept that our old selves have gone when we come into the knowledge of Christ Jesus our Lord. The old selves have no claim on us anymore. We must accept this truth within our hearts, so that we no longer can be moved by current or past problems or by what is happening around us.

Not only are we to cast our cares and worries onto Jesus, we must be balanced in our thinking, so that we won't be consumed by troubles. "Be well balanced (temperate, sober of mind), be vigilant and cautious at all times; for that enemy of yours, the devil, roams around like a lion roaring (in fierce hunger), seeking someone to seize upon and devour" (1 Peter 5:1–8 AMP). It is the enemy's plan to get you to continuously focus on what's wrong in your life, to be consumed by your problems, so that you will be distracted from doing God's will and worshipping the true and living God.

But to focus on anything other than God is what the Word calls "idol worship." We are to worship the Lord God Almighty and only him. If we focus on God the Father and his goodness, we cannot help but forget our troubles. One of the most important things I've learned is that the more we worship and focus on God, the more the light of God's spirit will empower us to overcome anything we have to face or that comes into our lives to destroy us. "I am the Lord your God who teaches you to profit, who leads you in the way that you should go" (Isaiah 48:17). If you worship God in the middle of your troubles, he will shine his light on you and show you the best way to move forward, if only you believe. God always provide a way of escape for his people (2 Corinthians 10:13).

Now, I'm not talking about walking around with your head in the sky and ignoring what's going on around you. What I'm saying is, don't give anything the power to control you or consume you. In other words, don't be consumed by the troubles in your life, but trouble your troubles by worshipping God. Yes, acknowledge the issues you are facing, but don't be consumed by them. Torment your trouble by acknowledging the power of your God, by continuously looking to the Lord. Worshipping God is looking to him, and when you worship, you will not worry. Instead of conducting negative worship (i.e., worrying), we are instructed to give all our anxieties to God, who cares for us "affectionately and watchfully." When we hand something over to God, we are saying, "God, I'm looking to you to handle this, and I trust that you can handle it totally." Looking to God for help is a form of worship. God takes pleasure in those who have faith in him, look to him for answers, and trust that he will not disappoint them.

Encouraging Scriptures for Meditation

"I will lift up mine eyes unto the hill, from where does my help come from? My help comes from the Lord, the Maker of heaven and earth. He will not let your foot slip, he who watches over you will not slumber; indeed, he who watches over Israel will neither slumber nor sleep. The Lord watches over you; the Lord is your shade at your right hand; the sun will not harm you by day, nor the moon by night. The lord will keep you from all harm he will watch over your life; the Lord will watch over your coming and going both now and forevermore." (Psalm 121)

"Let your character or moral disposition be free from the love of money including greed, avarice, lust and craving for earthly possessions and be satisfied with your present circumstances and with what you have; for he, God himself said, I will not in any way fail you nor give you up nor leave you helpless nor forsake nor let you down, relax my hold on you, assuredly not. So we take comfort and are encouraged and confidently and boldly say, the Lord is my

Helper, I will not be seized with alarm. I will not fear or dread or be terrified; what can man do to me?" (Hebrews 13:5–6 AMP)

"Trust in the Lord with all you heart and lean not on your own understanding and in all your ways acknowledge him and he will make your paths straight." (Proverbs 3:5–6)

"Therefore then, since we are surrounded by so great a cloud of witnesses who have borne testimony to the Truth, let us strip off and throw aside every encumbrance (unnecessary weight) and sin which so readily (deftly and cleverly) clings to and entangles us and lets run with patient endurance and steady and active persistence the appointed course of the race that is set before us, (looking away from all that will distract us and) focusing our eyes on Jesus, who is the Author and Finisher of faith (the first incentive for our belief and the One who brings our faith to maturity), who for the joy (of accomplishing the goal) set before Him endured the cross, disregarding the shame, and sat down at the right hand of the throne of God (revealing His deity, His authority, and the completion of His work)." (Hebrews 12:1–2 AMP)

"And therefore the Lord earnestly waits expecting looking, and longing to be gracious to you; therefore he lifts himself up, that he may have mercy on you and show loving kindness to you." (Isaiah 30:18)

Chapter 8

PRAYER: WORSHIPPING THROUGH THE POWER OF PRAYER

2 Chronicles 7:14
Mark 14:32–34
Luke 18:1–8
John 11:41–42
Acts 16:16–40
Romans 8:26, 12:12
Hebrews 4:15
Philippians 4:6
1 Corinthians 14:2
1 Thessalonians 5:17
Ephesians 6:18
James 5:13–18
1 Peter 3:12
Colossians 4:2

Prayer is another form of worship. But what is prayer,

really? Well, for the most part, we know prayer to be a form of communication with God the Father, when we talk to him. However, prayer is also listening, believing, and acting on God's plans for the earthly realm. Even when we feel we don't know how or what to pray for, God has promised to help us, because of his love for us. God loves us so much that his Spirit, which is inside us, will help us to pray.

> We do not know what we ought to pray for, but the Spirit himself intercedes for us with groans that words cannot express. And he who searches our hearts knows the mind of the spirit, because the spirit intercedes for the saints in accordance with God's will. (Romans 8:26)

The Word also tells us that God is a spirit, and a spirit can't operate in the earthly realm without a body, a physical form. When we pray, we give God the Father our permission to operate through us, to enter into any situation in which we need him to intervene. The Almighty Father needs his people to pray, to communicate with him continuously, to establish his will on the earth as it is in heaven.

> If my people, who are called by my name shall humble themselves, pray seek, crave and require of necessity my face and turn from their wicked ways, then will hear from heaven, forgiven their sin and heal their land. (2 Chronicles 7:14)

You have to talk to him. God hears the humble people, but he hates proud folk who are puffed up and will not call to him for help, guidance, understanding, and direction. He does not hear proud folk; he will resist them, and his ears are not attentive to their prayers. However, humble people who worship God through a life of prayer have made a very important choice that will empower them. A choice to worship God is a choice to turn away from sin; God said he would "heal their land." In other words, he will bless you; he will deliver and restore you; he will do whatever he needs to do to bring wholeness to your life. Either you will believe him or you will not—in the power of prayer.

One true fact we must realize is that God can only become involved in the affairs of our lives if we invite him to do so. The vehicle of prayer gives God access to our lives. Sometimes the Holy Spirit will help us communicate with God. Pray to him in the Spirit, which is also known as speaking in tongues—a way in which we talk to God in the spiritual realm. "For anyone who speaks in tongues does not speak to people but to God. Indeed, no one understands them; they utter mysteries by the Spirit" (1 Corinthians 14:2).

Other scriptural passages throughout the Word remind us of the importance of prayer:

"Is anyone of you in trouble? He should pray. Is anyone happy? Let him sing songs of praise. Is anyone of you sick? He should call the elders of the church to pray over him and anoint him with oil in the name of the Lord: the Lord will raise him up if he has sinned, he will be forgiven therefore confess your sins to each other and pray for each other so that you may be healed. The prayer of a righteous man is powerful and effective." (James 5:13–16)

"And pray in the Spirit on all occasions with all kinds of prayers and requests. With this in mind, be alert and always keep on praying for all the saints." (Ephesians 6:18)

"Be unceasing in prayer, praying perseveringly. Throughout the word of God men and women are encouraged, instructed and lead to pray and worship, especially during troubling and uncertain times." (1 Thessalonians 5:17)

"Devote yourselves to prayer, being watchful and thankful." (Colossians 4:2)

"For the eyes of the Lord are on the righteous; and his ears are attentive to their prayer, but the face of the Lord is against those who do evil." (1 Peter 3:12)

"Be joyful in hope, patient in affliction, faithful in prayer." (Romans 12:12)

"Do not be anxious about anything, but in everything by prayer and petition with thanksgiving present your requests to God." (Philippians 4:6)

Favorable Results through Prayer

In the midst of trouble, some people will feel as though there's no use in praying, or they will pray as a last resort.

Sometimes when the answer to their prayers seems to take too long to come, some will give up on their prayers and abandon their hope in God. However, when waiting for answers to prayers, one must operate in patience, endurance, and persistence. Being persistent in prayer will always bring favorable results. Take, for instance, the story of the persistent widow in Luke 18:1–8:

> Then Jesus told his disciples a parable to show them that they should always pray and not give up. He said: "in a certain town there was a judge who neither feared God nor cared about men. And there was a widow in the town that kept coming to him with the plea, 'grant me justice against my adversary.' For some time he refused. But finally he said to himself, even though I don't fear God or care about men, yet because this widow keeps bothering me, I will see that she gets justice, so that she won't eventually wear me out with her coming!" And the Lord said, "Listen to what the unjust judge says. And will not God bring about justice for his chosen one, who cries out to him day and night? Will see that they get justice and quickly. However, when the Son of Man comes, will he find faith on the earth?"

Some would like to believe that Jesus did not have

any problems or troubles in his life because he was the Son of God. However, because he was the Son of God, he had even more things to deal with and worry about. He carried the weight of the world on his shoulders, and no one can imagine how heavy that must have been. Any position of responsibility or authority, like being a parent or a supervisor, is challenging. Just stop and think: Jesus was responsible for humanity—now that's responsibility. Still, Jesus chose to worship and yield himself to God through unceasing prayer and communication with his Father.

> Then they went to a place called Gethsemane, and Jesus said to his disciples, "Sit here while I pray." And he took Peter, James, and John along with him, and he began to be deeply distressed and troubled. "My soul is overwhelmed with sorrow to the point of death," he said to them. "Stay here and keep watch." Going a little farther, he fell to the ground and prayed that if possible that the responsibility of the hour might pass from him. "Abba Father," he said, "everything is possible for you. Take this cup from me. Yet not what I will, but what you will." (Mark 14:32–34)

Father, Jesus said to himself, *this is hard, but your will be done.* At that moment, Jesus was facing the most difficult time in his life. He knew that the hour of his sacrificial death was near. Just the very thought of it could cause one to worry. But Jesus decided to worship and trust God the Father. I believe because Jesus worshipped instead of worried about what he was about to face, he was able to go through the horrible ordeal of suffering and remaining obedient until his death on the cross. But now he is glorified forever as he sits on the throne on the right-hand side of the Father in heaven, and the earth is his footstool.

Jesus, the most powerful man who ever walked on earth, demonstrated the importance and power of prayer. Just like we do, Jesus faced the problems, challenges, temptations, and the issues associated with daily living. But Jesus was able to overcome and live victoriously because he prayed continuously. In Hebrews 4:15 show us the human side of Jesus and the importance of prayer.

> For we do not have a high priest who is unable to sympathize with our weaknesses, but we have one who has been tempted in every way just as we are—yet was without sin. Let us then approach the throne of grace with confidence, so that we may receive mercy and find grace to help us in our time of need. (Hebrews 4:15)

Jesus had faith and confidence in the one to whom he was praying, God the Father. He was not hesitant, uncertain, or doubtful but was fully persuaded, just as Abraham was. I believe Jesus could approach the throne of grace with such confidence because of his faith in the Father. Even the tone of his prayer demonstrates how

51

to worship God. John 11:41–42 provides an excellent example of Jesus worshipping God confidently through prayer: Jesus faced the death of his dear friend Lazarus, but his faith and confidence in his heavenly Father were not shaken. He even thanked the Father for hearing and answering him: "Then Jesus looked up and said, 'Father I thank you that you have heard me. I know that you always hear me.'" Now that's faith, confidence, and worship at its best. Then he continued to pray: "but I said this for the benefit of the people standing here, that they may believe that you sent me."

Even though Jesus was the Son of God and possessed power and authority from on high, he still knew the importance of prayer. Because of the vehicle of prayer, we too have the same access to power and the authority to live a victorious life. Only if we practice the privilege of prayer will we experience the same victory and power Jesus possessed. Look at the prophet Elijah, who took advantage of a major move of God to change the circumstances of his life. He prayed a bold prayer that it would not rain, and it did not, James 5:17. Is there something in your life right now that needs a major move from God? Then get bold, and start praying. Because of God's love and the privilege of prayer, we too can boldly approach the throne of God with its advantages and many privileges. Countless men and women have discovered the art of worshipping the Father through prayer instead of living a life of worry.

Finally, there are other benefits and privileges to prayer. For one, there are no boundaries in prayer. It can be done anywhere, anytime, by anyone for any reason, person, place, or thing. Now that is awesome. Because there are no boundaries in prayer, a lot more of us should have tapped into living a blessed life, regardless of the problems associated with daily living. In Acts 16:16–40, the apostles Paul and Silas are in prison, facing death. But look at the boldness of the church members who prayed earnestly to God for them. While they were praying, Paul and the others worshipped God from a prison cell. Paul experienced the miracle of walking out of prison from the clutches of the evil King Herod, who wanted to destroy him; because Paul's church members approached the throne of grace on his behalf, not only was he released from prison, he was able to witness and win souls for the kingdom of God. Just think; we can experience miracles because of our earnest prayers and worship. We have access to God the Father anywhere, anytime, for any reason. Our heavenly Father loves us so much; he made himself available to us—always. I can't think of anyone or anything else with such power and authority to whom we have that much access.

Chapter 9

RESTORATION: IS IT POSSIBLE?

2 Kings 8:1–6
Joel 2:25
Psalm 23:3, 42:1–2, 107:1–7
2 Chronicles 15:15

After facing adversity in life, most people want to know one thing: is restoration possible for me? However, many people will never admit that they are facing adversity because they have totally ignored God and his will. It pays to serve God, to be his child, to do his will; we can avoid all kinds of trouble. Unfortunately, some of us only learn to do better after we have been through a great deal. It is also unfortunate that some may go through life without ever looking for restoration, because they don't know that restoration is available to them. But God promises restoration for the weary. Throughout the Word of God, we see restoration given to all sorts of people—some deserving, some not. God is full of grace and mercy; even when we don't deserve his goodness and forgiveness, he has the grace to restore us. Today, we can be confident and stand on God's promises for restoration.

"He restores my soul. He guides me in paths of righteousness for his name's sake" (Psalm 23:3). In this fallen world, we all need an overhaul in the soul-is realm from time to time. In the center of our souls is where we feel, think and want. And from time to time we need to keep a watchful eye on our souls, through the Word of God and prayer. In the realm of the soul, we should desire more and more to please God—to want what he wants, to think as he does, to follow his Word, and to want to do his will in the earthly realm. However, if we do not yield to him, our souls will become more worldly and displeasing to God. The more we fill our hearts and minds with the Word of God, the more we will operate in line with it.

The question is, with what are you feeding your soul? "As the deer pants and thirst for streams of water, so my soul pants and thirst for you, my God. My soul thirsts for the living God," Psalm 42:1–2. That was King David, who spoke about thirsting after God with all of his soul. The Lord promises to restore us totally:

> I will restore to you the years that the locust hath eaten, the cankerworm and the caterpillar and the palmerworm, my great army which I sent among you. And ye shall eat in plenty and be satisfied and praise the name of the Lord your God that have dealt

> wondrously with you; and my people shall never be ashamed. And ye shall know that I am in the midst of Israel and the name of the Lord your God, and none else: and my people shall never be ashamed. (Joel 2:25)

Not only does God the Father restore our souls, he redeems them as well. He brought our souls back from the enemy when we faced nothing but death, destruction, and eternal damnation. By shedding his blood, Jesus brought our soul back from the enemy, so that makes us the "redeemed" of the Lord. This is why I love Psalm 107:1–7:

> Oh give thanks to the Lord, for he is good; for is mercy; and loving kindness endure forever! Let the redeemed of the Lord say so, whom he has delivered from the hand of the adversary and gathered them out of the land, from the east and the south. Some wandered in the wilderness in solitary desert track they found no city for habitation. Hungry and thirsty they fainted; their lives were near to being extinguished. Then they cried to the Lord in their trouble, and he delivered them out of their distresses. He lead them forth by the straight and right way, that they might go to a city a where they could establish their homes.

When the children of Israel decided to turn back to God, he healed them. He told them he would restore them, and he did. At one time the children of Israel had left God and his counsel, and things began to go wrong for them. Some of us, when things go wrong, we wonder what's going on in our lives. But once the Israelites made up their minds to turn back to God and to the things of God, he restored them again.

I believe that is just what some of us need to do—totally submit to God. Turn back to him and let your lifestyle worship him. My friend, if you find yourself in a situation that's destroying your life, check yourself and evaluate your life to see if you are out of order with God in certain areas. Then make a quality decision to turn back to him and away from the destructive lifestyle. Sometimes we get ourselves in trouble by rebelling against God the Father. But if you just turn back to the Lord, he promises to heal you and restore your life.

> The spirit of God came upon Azariah, son of Oded. He went out to meet Asa and said to him, "Listen to me Asa and all Judah and Benjamin. The Lord is with you as long as you are with him. If you seek him, he will be found by you, but if you forsake him, he will forsake you. For a long time Israel was without the true God, without a priest to teach and without the law. But in their distress they turned to the Lord, the God

of Israel and sought him and he was found by them." (2 Chronicles 15:15)

A Perfect Example of Restoration

Now Elisha had said to the woman whose son he had restored to life, "Go away with your family and stay for a while wherever you can, because the Lord has decreed a famine in the land that will last seven year." The woman proceeded to do as the man of God said. She and her family went away and stayed in the land of the Philistines seven years. At the end of the seven years she came back from the land of the Philistines and went to the king to beg for her house and said, "Tell me about all the great things Elisha has done." Just as Gehazi was telling the king how Elisha had restored the dead to life, the woman came in to beg the king for her house and land. Gehazi said, "My lord and king this is the woman and her son whom Elisha restored to life." The king asked the woman about it, and she told him. "Give back everything that belonged to her," [the king said,] "including all the income from her land from the day she left the country until now." (2 Kings 8:1–6 NIV)

This is a perfect example of how God restores his children. Not only did he restore what the woman lost originally, but he gave her interest and more than she had lost. Now that is what I call restoration. One can't help but worship such a loving, kind, caring, and just God. We will realize how much God really loves us when we stop looking for him to bless, deliver, heal, and restore us the way we want him to. We must trust the all-knowing God to do what he knows to be best. We must remember that God knows all things—the beginning, the end, and everything in-between. The problem is, we are limited in our ability to comprehend the Lord's plan for our lives. Even if we mess up, and we will, the Word promises that all things work together for our good, for those who love, trust, and are called for his purpose (Romans 8:28).

Chapter 10

I CHOOSE TO WORSHIP: MY CHOICE, MY LIFESTYLE

Psalms 118:24, 51:10
Philippines 2:1–5, 3:7–14, 4:10–13
Colossians 2:6–15
Genesis 4:3–9
2 Timothy 1:7
2 Corinthians 10:5

Worrying causes us to live a life less than what God has planned for us. Furthermore, feelings of grief, pain, hatred, jealousy, offense, and hurt can keep us from glorifying God in our daily lives. But we have the power and the ability of choice to rule over all our feelings and attitudes of the heart, even destructive feelings. We choose what attitude resides in our heart. We must remember that "... God did not give us a spirit of timidity *or* cowardice *or* fear, but [He has given us a spirit] of power and of love and of sound judgment *and* personal discipline [abilities that result in a calm, well-balanced mind and self-control]" (2 Timothy 1:7)

Our heavenly Father also gave us a spirit of "power, love and a sound mind." Therefore, we do not have to accept any feelings other than love, power, and soundness of mind. We should realize and acknowledge that God does not send feelings of fear, hopelessness, and destructive weariness; so when they rise up within us, we should immediately cast them out. The enemy uses destructive spirits to destroy us. John 10:10 clearly tell us that Jesus came to give us an abundant life, but the devil comes to "kill, steal, and destroy us and our lives any way he can." Just as God is a spirit of "power and love," the enemy is also a spirit, and he will assign other spirits to kill, steal from, and destroy us. But we have power over what dwells inside us. The power of God dwells in us. We have power. "We demolish arguments and every pretension that sets itself up against the knowledge of God, and we take captive every thought to make it obedient to Christ" (2 Corinthians 10:5). You see, friend, we demolish and we take captive those spirits, feelings, and thoughts. In 2 Corinthians 10:5, God is telling us to take back our power and change our attitudes by choosing what has permission to dwell in us. If I were you, I would choose to worship. Immediately get rid of anything inside you that God did not send. I do believe that simply focusing on and worshipping God will rid you of negative and destructive feelings. When we usher in the presence of the Lord, we are guaranteed peace, joy, love, and victory over the enemies of life.

Remember when Cain killed his brother, Abel? He did

not have to do that; he had a choice, an opportunity to present God with a sacrificial offering in faith, just as Abel had. God even warned Cain that sin was crouching at his door, waiting for him to bow down to it, but he didn't have to submit to it. What rose up in Cain's heart—jealousy, hatred, murder—will come to us all. But we have the power to choose. James 3:16 says, "Where jealousy and strife are, every evil work is present." Now God gave Cain the power to rule over what was in his heart. But Cain chose to operate in the spirit of jealousy rather than offer a gift to God in faith (Genesis 4:3–9). We honor God when we operate in faith. It takes faith to make a decision to worship, because as life happens, you will not feel like operating in faith. God gave Cain the power to choose worship, but he chose not to. The enemy will use anything to distract you from a life of faith. We must be mindful of these destructive feelings of the heart and stop allowing them to linger. Above all else, we must continually protect our hearts, because from our hearts flow our feelings and attitudes (Proverbs 4:23). When we trust and honor God more than we do our own feelings and experiences, we have strength to move on. We can even worship God from a wounded, troubled, or uncertain place. The Father can deliver us from anywhere in the spiritual realm, as long as we turn to him in faith. Even that is worship.

When you are having a bad day or if things don't seem to be working in your favor, your attitude must be "This is the day that the Lord has made. I choose to be glad in it" (Psalm 118:24). I choose to be kind-hearted when people are not so nice to me. I choose to be faithful when life presents disappointment. I choose to be prosperous when I am faced with obstacles. I choose to be blessed and a blessing to others. I choose to go higher with the power of God Almighty despite what comes up against me. I choose to worship God as I express and experience life one day at a time. Stay focused, and get back on track. "Oh God create in me a clean heart and renew a right/ steadfast spirit within me" (Psalm 51:10). Remember the enemy is after your worship, your faith, and your attention. Who do you honor? To whom do you submit? Who are you worshipping, because it really is your choice?

Chapter 11

THE REDEEMED LIFE: A LIFESTYLE THAT WORSHIPS GOD

Hebrews 12
John 15:4-5
Romans 6:6–10, 8:31–39
Colossians 3:5–15
2 Corinthians 12:9

To live as redeemed people in a fallen world we must first realize, understand and know Jesus Christ and our position in him. In this life, we often face problems, troubles, and hindrances in that will try to destroy us. But we can persevere if we remember that we belong to God the Father, pursue a lifestyle of worship, and continuously look to Jesus—our rock, our strength, and the author and finisher of our faith. Jesus also reminds us that we can do nothing if we are apart from him, not even live a Christian life that will glorify the Father. We must remain in Christ to live a victorious life (John 15:4–5). When we don't stay focused on Jesus Christ, we lose our way.

How can we live as redeemed people in a fallen world? First, we have to know who we are, to know beyond a shadow of doubt that we are redeemed and the old man is gone, buried, and hidden in Christ Jesus (Romans 6:6–10). Once people know that the old man has been crucified with Christ Jesus, they can live a redeemed life. In other words, to know a thing is to accept it, to allow it to happen, to believe it, and to receive it. I decided that I was made new in Christ; that was my choice. Once a person allows the old man to die, the new man can begin to live for God the Father. When a person lives a lifestyle of worship, he stops opening the door of his heart to the old self and puts that old self to death. He lives the life of a new man, thanks to his faith in Jesus Christ, who delivers us from that former life that did not glorify God. Redeemed people purposely live as God's chosen people, glorifying him in their daily lives.

Second, we live as redeemed people because God's grace gives us power to do so in this fallen world. Our redemption was bought with the blood of Jesus Christ, which was shed for us so we could have the gift of eternal life and the forgiveness of sins. As the Bible reminds us, God's power rests on us so that we will be redeemed. We cannot lose that redemption, and no one can take it away. God really did so love the world, his creation, that he redeemed us through the shed blood of his Son, Jesus Christ (John 3:16).

We Are More than Conquerors

What, then, shall we say in response to these things? If God is for us, who can be against us? He who did not spare his own Son, but gave him up for us all—how will he not also, along with him, graciously give us all things? Who will bring any charge against those whom God has chosen? It is God who justifies. Who then is the one who condemns no one? Christ Jesus who died—more than that, who was raised to life—is at the right hand of God and is also interceding for us. Who shall separate us from the love of Christ? Shall trouble or hardship or persecution or famine or nakedness or danger or sword? As it is written; "For your sake we face death all day long; we are considered as sheep to be slaughtered." No, in all these things we are more than conquerors through him who loved us. For I am convinced that neither death nor life, neither angels nor demons, neither the present nor the future nor any powers, neither height nor depth, nor anything else in all creation, will be able to separate us from the love of God that is in Christ Jesus our Lord. (Romans 8:31–39)

Prayer and Instruction for a Redeemed Life

Dear friend, in order to possess the kingdom of God here on earth and be in covenant with God, you must first come to know and understand the heavenly Father through a personal relationship with his Son, Jesus Christ. The only way to have this relationship is to accept Jesus Christ as your personal Lord and Savior. You can do this by believing that Jesus Christ is Lord, confessing your sins, and purposely turning away from a lifestyle characterized by sin, death, and damnation. Surrender your life to God by reciting this simple prayer and allowing him to fill your heart with the His Holy Spirit:

> "Father, in the name of Jesus, I recognize and acknowledge that I am a sinner. I now repent and purposely turn from a life of sin, death and destruction. I confess with my mouth and believe in my heart that Jesus Christ is Lord and that you raised him from the dead. I invite you Lord Jesus to come into my heart and into my life and fill me with your Holy Spirit and with your love. Thank you, Lord, for saving me. Amen." Romans 10:9–10

Welcome to the family of God. Ephesians 2:19 tells us that we are "no longer foreigners and aliens, but fellow citizens with God's people and members of God's household." Now that you have prayed and confessed, I pray that you will develop a strong spiritual life. Pray, study, and obey God's Word daily; be joyful and purposefully walk in love (2 Timothy 3:16, 1 Thessalonians 5:16–18). Join a good Bible-believing church. Be faithful and committed in a church that doesn't let anything or anyone to turn you back (Hebrews 10:25). Get baptized by water (Matthew 3:6). Pray and ask the Holy Spirit to baptize you, using the evidence of speaking in tongues (Acts 2:3–4). Remember that God's love will never fail you (John 3:16, 2 Corinthians 13:8).

If you fall in your daily walk with God, remember his love, get up, and repent by purposefully turning away from sin and keep on walking with God.

In This Season, Stay Focused and Flexible

Worship will always shift the atmosphere in your favor. When we cry out in worship, our valley of dry bones will come alive. The enemy has to shut his mouth as we continuously walk in victory in any and every season of life. For when the enemy comes up against us, to hinder and disparage our gifts, our worship will stop him in his tracks. Our worship will always be our weapon for breaking the back of the enemy. Troubles and problems may come to destroy us, but through our worship, we can witness our abundant victory on a greater level. If we do not faint during our season of testing and trying, we will reap blessings due to a shift in the atmosphere because of our worship.

Appendix

Scripture References That Will Bless Your Life
2 Corinthians 4:8, 5:17–18, 10:5, 13
John 5:38–40, 14:1, 23–24
Mark 24:4
Romans 8:2
Hebrews 12:1–2, 13:5–6
Judges 10:13
James 1:2-18, 2:1, 22–25
Luke 4:8
Psalms 34:19, 42:5, 51:10, 55:22, 91, 138:8
Colossians 1:13, 27
Proverbs 5:18, 10:24
Philippians 4:4–8
Job 23:1
Jeremiah 29:11

Printed in the United States
By Bookmasters